WHAT IS SHONEN JUMP?

SHONEN JUMP is the birthplace of manga stars Yugi, Ken, Arale and Senbei, as well as continuing hits *RUROUNI KENSHIN, BLEACH, DRAGON BALL Z* and *THE PRINCE OF TENNIS*. Originating in Japan, each issue of Japan's *Shonen Jump Weekly* carries the decades-long tradition of Japanese comics propelled by vibrant art and intriguing storylines. Now that VIZ has brought the *SHONEN JUMP* magazine to the U.S., American readers can discover what millions of manga fans already know: no other comic packs more action and adventure between its covers.

Capture it first in SHONEN JUMP MAGAZINE!
Subscribe now at www.shonenjump.com

WHAT IS THE SHONEN JUMP GRAPHIC NOVEL LINE?

The *SHONEN JUMP GRAPHIC NOVEL* line is the future of manga — it's the voice of the most exciting titles making the leap from Japan to the U.S.

Each manga title has the unique style and voice of its artist/creator. All of the manga are presented in the right-to-left format just as they are in Japan. The format allows the panels to be displayed as the artists intended, and adds authenticity and fun to the reader's experience.

So brace yourself for an amazing experience as you read through the fourth *SHONEN JUMP GRAPHIC NOVEL COMPILATION EDITION*. Here's a sample of the intense action, nail-biting cliffhangers and coolest characters around. You're about to JUMP head first into the world of manga. Enjoy!

THE WORLD'S
ST POPULAR MANGA

GRAPHIC NOVELS

Managing Editor *Elizabeth Kawasaki*
Cover *Courtney Utt*
Graphic Design *Izumi Hirayama*

Vice President & Editor in Chief *Yumi Hoashi*
Vice President of Publishing *Alvin Lu*
Director of Production *Noboru Watanabe*
Sr. Director of Acquisitions *Rika Inouye*
Vice President of Sales & Marketing *Liza Coppola*
Publisher *Hyoe Narita*

DR. SLUMP

STORY & ART BY *AKIRA TORIYAMA*
Translation & English Adaptation *Alexander O. Smith*
Touch-Up & Lettering *Walden Wong*
Graphics & Cover Design *Sean Lee*
Editor *Yuki Takagaki*

LEGENDZ

ART BY *MAKOTO HARUNO*
STORY BY *RIN HIRAI*
Translation *Akira Watanabe*
English Adaptation *Shaenon K. Garrity*
Touch-Up Art & Lettering *Susan Daigle-Leach*
Graphics & Cover Design *Sean Lee*
Editor *Yuki Takagaki*

YU-GI-OH!: DUELIST

STORY & ART BY *KAZUKI TAKAHASHI*
Translation & English Adaptation *Joe Yamazaki*
Touch-Up & Lettering *Jim Keefe*
Graphics & Cover Design *Sean Lee*
Editor *Jason Thompson*

YU-GI-OH!: MILLENNIUM WORLD

STORY & ART BY *KAZUKI TAKAHASHI*
Translation & English Adaptation *Anita Sengupta*
Touch-Up Art & Lettering *Kelle Han*
Graphics & Cover Design *Sean Lee*
Editor *Jason Thompson*

Printed in the U.S.A.

www.shonenjump.com

EXPLANATION OF AGE RATINGS

 ALL AGES Suitable for all ages. May contain some violence. Example: *Legendz*

 TEEN May contain violence, language, suggestive situations and alcohol or tobacco usage. Recommended for ages 13 and up. Examples: *Dr. Slump*, *Yu-Gi-Oh!: Duelist* and *Yu-Gi-Oh!: Millennium World*

CONTENTS

Duel Monsters is the world's most popular collectible card game—but to Yugi Mutou, whose body contains the spirit of the world's greatest gamer, it may be the most dangerous game he's ever played! A mysterious videotape sends Yugi and his friends to Duelist Kingdom, the island home of super-rich American game designer Maximillion Pegasus. There, Yugi must compete with the world's greatest Duel Monsters players… but this is no ordinary tournament. The path of the duelist will lead Yugi face to face with the other owners of the Millennium Items…gamers with powers equal to his own!

DUEL 1: CHALLENGE!!!

BANG

DUEL MONSTERS!!

MOUNTAIN WARRIOR

A TRADING CARD GAME WHERE PLAYERS BECOME WIZARDS WHO SUMMON MONSTERS AND CAST SPELLS TO DO BATTLE!

EVERYONE IN MY CLASS PLAYS THIS GAME AT RECESS.

...I USE THE SPELL CARD *WIND OF THE GODS*!

WSSH

THE HOLY WIND ERODES YOUR GOLEM! HE TURNS TO DUST AND BLOWS AWAY!

I WIN!

ROCK OGRE GROTTO #1

ATK/800 DEF/1200

LOOK HOW STRONG HE IS!

I ATTACK WITH *ROCK OGRE GROTTO*!

BWA HA HA! TAKE THIS, ANZU!

THEN ON *MY* TURN...

GO FOR IT, ANZU!

WHAT AM I DOING WRONG?!

SHAKE

SHAKE

YUGI! WHY... WHY?! WHY CAN'T I WIN?

YOU'RE SO *LAME*, JONOUCHI!

AGGGH! I LOST AGAIN ?!

GONG

JONOUCHI LIFE POINTS 0

HERE!

SHOW ME YOUR DECK, JONOUCHI!

THE BIGGEST STRATEGY IN THIS GAME IS *COMBINING* MONSTERS AND SPELL CARDS!

YOUR OPPONENT CAN *EASILY* DODGE YOUR ATTACKS IF YOU FIGHT WITH YOUR MONSTERS ALONE!

HEH HEH! THAT'S RIGHT! I STUFFED MY DECK WITH THE STRONGEST MONSTERS I COULD FIND!

UH... THAT'S NO GOOD!

ACK! WHAT'S THIS !?

TADA

YOUR WHOLE DECK'S MADE OF MONSTERS ?! ALL 40 CARDS?!

HMMMM... MM... ☆

...YOU'VE CHOSEN A **GREAT** TIME! THE FINALS OF THE DUEL MONSTERS TOURNAMENT IS ON TV AT 5:00 TONIGHT!

LET'S WATCH IT TOGETHER!

IT *IS?*

OKAY! COME BY MY PLACE AFTER SCHOOL!

OH, AND...

PLEASE! YOU GOTTA TRAIN ME TO PLAY BETTER!

AWRIGHT, YUGI!

GRAB

HUH, YOU CLOSED ALREADY?

HO HO! OF COURSE!

THE DUEL MONSTERS FINALS ARE TONIGHT! I CAN'T BE STUCK WATCHING THE SHOP!

AH, YUGI! WELCOME HOME!

YOU'RE ALL HERE! COME ON IN!

I'M HOME, GRANDPA!

HIYA!

HO HO...

CLOSED

CLATTER

10

THAT'S MY DREAM!

THIS TIME FAIR AND SQUARE!

YUP!

YOU MEAN KAIBA...

I STILL...

I WENT TO VISIT HIM YESTERDAY... NO CHANGE...

...IN THE HOSPITAL. HE HASN'T WOKEN UP YET.

I HEAR KAIBA'S STILL...

NEVER!

I'D NEVER TRUST THAT CREEP!

EVEN IF HE CAME BACK, I STILL WOULDN'T TRUST HIM!

RAAA

DUEL MONSTERS TOURNAMENT FINALS

OHO! IT'S ABOUT TO START!

FOR THE THOUSANDS OF DUEL MONSTERS FANS ACROSS THE COUNTRY, IT ALL COMES DOWN TO *THIS* MOMENT!

THE FINAL ROUND OF THE DUEL MONSTERS TOURNAMENT IS ABOUT TO BEGIN!

THE FINALISTS ARE ENTERING THE STADIUM!

OUT OF THE *200* DUELISTS WHO MADE IT THROUGH THE REGIONALS TO THIS TOURNAMENT, ONLY *ONE* CAN CLAIM THE CROWN!

FROM WEST JAPAN! *"DINOSAUR"* RYUZAKI! FIFTEEN YEARS OLD!

FROM EAST JAPAN! *"INSECTOR"* HAGA! FOURTEEN YEARS OLD!

NOW THE DUELISTS ARE IN THE DUEL BOX! THEY'RE SITTING DOWN!

THIS VIRTUAL SIMULATION BOX WAS DEVELOPED BY INDUSTRIAL ILLUSIONS, THE MAKERS OF DUEL MONSTERS, IN COOPERATION WITH KAIBA CORP!

OOOOOO

WooO

LET THE BATTLE BEGIN!

WHATEVER! MY DINOSAUR CARDS WILL *CRUSH* YOU LIKE AN *ANT!*

I CAN HEAR YOUR CARDS SHAKING IN FEAR...

DUEL!

SNP FWP

RAAAA

HEY YUGI! WHO YOU THINK'S GONNA WIN?

THE DINO-SAUR'S GOTTA WIN!

IF IT'S BETWEEN *INSECTS* AND *DINOSAURS*, THEN THERE'S NO QUESTION!

HE'LL ATTACK BY ENHANCING HIS INSECT CARDS WITH ARMOR CARDS AND STUFF!

INSECTOR HAGA'S SPECIALTY IS *INSECT COMBOS!!*

ON THE OTHER SIDE, DINOSAUR RYUZAKI USES THE MEGATON POWER OF HIS DINOSAUR CARDS TO *OVERWHELM* HIS ENEMY!

THERE THEY GO! LOOK!

YOU THINK SO...?

DOOMM

DINOSAUR RYUZAKI HAS PLAYED HIS RARE CARD, THE MOST POWERFUL OF THE DINOSAURS, *TWO-HEADED KING REX!*

TAKE THAT !!

......

TH-THANK YOU!

CONGRATULATIONS!

UH...

YOU JUST *MUST* COME TO THE TOURNAMENT MY COMPANY WILL BE SPONSORING!

NOW I GET WHAT YOU SAID ABOUT HOW EVEN STRONG MONSTERS CAN'T STAND AGAINST A GOOD *COMBO*!

WATCHING THAT GOT ME ALL FIRED UP!

INSECTOR HAGA, EH...? CAN'T SAY I'M SURPRISED.

ALTHOUGH THE EXCITEMENT IS STILL RUNNING HIGH IN THE STADIUM, WE MUST SIGN OFF FOR NOW! DON'T FORGET TO COLLECT ALL THE LIMITED EDITION DUEL MONSTERS TOURNAMENT CARDS AT DUEL CENTERS NEAR YOU!

OKAY !!

C'MON YUGI! TRAIN ME! TRAIN ME!

ME NEITHER! BUT IT SURE WAS A GREAT DUEL!

RAAA

Panazonic

WHA...!?

BEFORE YOU DO THAT, YUGI...

I'D LIKE TO KNOW WHAT'S IN THIS PACKAGE...

WONDER WHAT IT IS?

WE CAN PLAY AFTER I OPEN THIS!

OH YEAH...

I FORGOT...

A STRANGE GLOVE... WITH STAR-SHAPED CHIPS?!?!

AND AN 8MM VIDEOTAPE... WHAT IN THE WORLD...?!

BANG

WHAT THE--?!

YUP! WE HAVE AN 8MM PLAYER!

CAN YOU PLAY IT, YUGI?

IS ON THIS TAPE!

MAYBE THE EXPLANATION ...

OKAY, LET'S SEE!

!!

K·ZZSSS

NICE TO MEET YOU!

AT LAST WE MEET, YUGI-BOY!

VMMM

HELLO!

Panasonic

THE **AMERICAN** WAS JUST ON TV... THE GUY WHO **CREATED** DUEL MONSTERS! PEGASUS SOMETHING!!

THAT'S THE GUY WHO...!

AFTER ALL... YOU **DEFEATED** KAIBA-BOY!

I UNDERSTAND YOU ARE **VERY** SKILLED AT DUEL MONSTERS!

GOOD JOB! WELL DONE! **WON**DERFUL!

VIDEO **LETTER**?!

I JUST WANTED TO SEND A VIDEO LETTER TO THE **ESTEEMED** YUGI-BOY, THE **REAL** CHAMPION!

NO, NO! DON'T BE SO SURPRISED!

!!

I CHALLENGE YOU TO FACE THIS **VIDEO RECORDING** OF ME AT DUEL MONSTERS!

WHAT ?!!

NOW, SHALL WE GET DOWN TO BUSINESS, YUGI-BOY?

I WANT TO TEST YOUR SKILL RIGHT HERE AND NOW!

HE CAN'T EVEN KNOW WHAT CARDS YUGI PLAYS?!

IMPOSSIBLE!! THAT'S NO CHALLENGE!

HOW CAN YUGI PLAY AGAINST SOMEONE RECORDED ON A VIDEOTAPE...!

IN FIVE MINUTES, OUR DUEL WILL BEGIN!

BUILD YOUR DECK IN FRONT OF THE MONITOR!

ALL RIGHT?

DUEL!

ARE YOU READY? THEN LET'S GO!

SHP

OKAY! I'LL TAKE ANY CHALLENGE!

I'LL DO IT!

YOU GONNA DO IT, YUGI?

KOUMORI DRAGON

VSH

OKAY!

OKAY! MY DECK IS READY!

MY OPPONENT'S THE CREATOR OF DUEL MONSTERS! TO PLAY AGAINST HIM IS A DREAM!

I'LL START WITH THE KOUMORI DRAGON-- THE DEVIL DRAGON CARD!

HOW CAN HE SEE THE CARDS FROM ACROSS THE SCREEN!

THIS CAN'T BE...!

WHAT...?!

LET ME GUESS... THE KOUMORI DRAGON, RIGHT...?

YOU'RE PLANNING TO COMBINE THE KOUMORI DRAGON WITH THE DRAGON KNIGHT ON YOUR NEXT TURN TO INCREASE YOUR ATTACK POWER! AM I WRONG?

YOU SEE, YUGI-BOY... I *KNEW* THAT YOU WERE GOING TO PLAY THAT CARD!

WHY, I EVEN KNOW WHAT'S IN YOUR HAND!

HE JUST GUESSED THE NAME OF MY CARD...?!

RMMBB!!

DEVIL DRAGON SEALED!!

HEH HEH... WE CAN'T HAVE THAT... SO I'LL REMOVE YOUR KOUMORI DRAGON WITH MY DRAGON CAPTURE JAR!

!!

NO WAY...! CAN HE READ MY MIND?!

RMMB

THEN I'LL BE YOUR OPPONENT!

DON'T MESS WITH ME!

THIS IS...

RMMB

THIS ISN'T GOING TO BE EASY...

...A SHADOW GAME!!

THE PICTURE ON THE CARD...

...GOT SUCKED INTO THE TV SCREEN!!

HEH HEH...

I'M FIGHTING THE MAN WHO MADE THE GAME!

Return to the world where it all began!

Millennium World

SHONEN JUMP GRAPHIC NOVEL

Story & Art by
Kazuki Takahashi volume **1**

- 3 times yearly
- $7.95
- Volume 1 available in August!
- Serialized in SHONEN JUMP

After hundreds of battles, Yugi has finally gathered all the Egyptian God Cards...the key to unlocking his memories of his past life as an Egyptian pharaoh. When Ryo Bakura gives him the Millennium Eye, Yugi opens the door to the "world of memory," and his mind travels back in time to ancient Egypt, when the magic and monsters were real! Now Yugi and his friends must explore the world of Yugi's forgotten past...and fight an enemy who has been waiting for them for 3,000 years!

Duel 5: The Six Chosen Priests

Duel 5: The Six Chosen Priests

URGH ...

FOR A MOMENT THERE WAS THIS BRIGHT LIGHT...

WHAT IN THE WORLD IS GOIN' ON?

HEY YUGI! ARE YOU OKAY?

YUGI!!!

...

WHERE DID YOU GO?

UHH...

HE'S GONE?!

OTHER ME, WHERE ARE YOU?

NO WAY...

THE PHARAOH HAS GONE TO THE WORLD OF HIS MEMORY...

THE WORLD OF MEMORY...!

SHWO

WH-WHAT ARE YOU SAYING?!

GREAT PHARAOH...

WHERE AM I...?

...!

MM..

OH, THE SHAME OF IT...!

IN ALL TIMES, YOU MUST ACT WITH DIGNITY AS BEFITS THE LIVING REPRESENTATION OF THE GODS!

TO FALL **ASLEEP** ON THE THRONE ...!

"GRANDPA"?! I HAVE **NEVER** BEEN CALLED BY ANY OTHER NAME!

IT IS I, YOUR VIZIER, SIAMUN MURAN.

GR.. ?!

...?!

GRANDPA!!

SIAMUN ...

...!!

WHAT'S GOING ON...?

...?!

"PHARAOH" ...?!

WHY AM I DRESSED LIKE THIS...?!

...IT IS TIME.

O GREAT PHARAOH...

WHO IN THE WORLD ARE THESE GUYS...?

WHAT?!

I MEAN... SIAMUN... WHAT'S GOING ON HERE?

HEY, GR...

HUH...?!

...

WHAT DO YOU MEAN?

...

THEY ALL HAVE MILLENNIUM ITEMS!

THE SIX PRIESTS... CHOSEN BY THE MILLENNIUM ITEMS?

THESE ARE THE SIX HIGH PRIESTS CHOSEN BY THE MILLENNIUM ITEMS!

WE ARE ABOUT TO BEGIN THE ROYAL COURT...

YES, YOUR MAJESTY ...AS YOU KNOW...

THE PHARAOH MUST BE VERY TIRED...

BRING IN THE PRISONER!!

GREAT PHARAOH! MAY WE OPEN THE COURT?

NO... WAIT...

THIS WAY!

!!

V-VERY WELL...

THE TOMB WAS EMPTY WHEN I GOT THERE! THERE WAS NO TREASURE, NOT EVEN--

I'M NOT A THIEF! I DIDN'T STEAL ANYTHING!

BE QUIET!

GRR...

THIS MAN WAS CAUGHT TRYING TO ENTER THE TOMB OF THE FORMER PHARAOH!

GGK...

LEARN NOW THAT THOSE WHO SET FOOT IN THE SACRED GROUND WILL FACE THE GODS' JUDGMENT!

THE RESTING PLACE OF THE PHARAOHS IS THE TERRITORY OF THE GODS!!

THE MILLENNIUM ITEMS!

THESE *SINNERS* ARE JUDGED BY THE SEVEN HOLY ITEMS OF THE PHARAOH AND THE SIX PRIESTS...

GREAT PHARAOH...

THERE IS NO END TO THIEVES LIKE THIS, WHO WOULD ROB THE ROYAL TOMBS...

TO JUDGE THE SINNERS?

IS *THAT* WHAT THE MILLENNIUM ITEMS ARE FOR...?!

NOW YOUR CRIME WILL BE JUDGED BY THE SEVEN MILLENNIUM ITEMS!!

THE SIX PRIESTS CHOSEN BY THE **POWER OF ONE THOUSAND YEARS** HAVE THE ABILITY TO EXORCISE THESE DEMONS...

...AND *SEAL THEM AWAY* IN STONE SLABS!

STONE SLABS ...?!

The Birth of Arale!

*NORIMAKI SENBEI: A RICE CRACKER WRAPPED IN SEAWEED

ZZZZZT
ZZZZZT

SNUFFLE,
SNUFFLE
...

YAWN.

WHEW
...

HMM.
SHOULD'VE
PUT THE
TALKING BITS
ON LAST.

BO-RING.

52

HOW ABOUT A TUMMY MISSILE? *BAZOOOM!*

NO.

WHO SAID ANYTHING ABOUT FIGHTING EVIL!?

THEN WHAT WILL I USE TO FIGHT THE FORCES OF EVIL?

FEMININE CHARM...?

HUH?

ARE MY EYES BAD?

WHAT NOW?

HEY.

GAH! THIS WON'T DO!

DOCTOR, YOUR FACE LOOKS ALL GOOFY.

53

54

WAIT HERE. I'LL GO BUY YOU SOME CLOTHES.

GOING OUT, DOCTOR?

CAN'T HAVE YOU WEARING MY PJs FOREVER.

WHO TAUGHT YOU THAT?

A MINK COAT?

LET'S SEE... GOT THAT, THAT...

WHAT'S LEFT?

THE STORE

50% OFF

THE STORE

EVERYTHING HALF OFF

DIAPERS & MISSILES IN STOCK!!

UNDER-WEAR.

A-HA! I KNOW!

BLAST! THEY'LL THINK I'M A PERVERT FOR SURE!

LOOK, IT'S NOT FOR ME! IT'S A PRESENT FOR MY MOTHER!

I HAVE A DRESS THAT WOULD LOOK SPLENDID ON YOU, SIR.

HEH HEH. FOR THE MISSUS, YOU KNOW.

...AND LIPSTICK?

SWOOSH

THANK YOU! COME AGAIN!

AH! I KNOW JUST THE THING.

POP

SKRIK
SKRIK

TOILET

WELCOME!

= WOMEN   = MEN

BLAST! THIS IS PATHETIC!

SQUEAK
SQUEAK

MMMPH

FORGET IT, BUDDY. YOU AIN'T MY TYPE.

WHO GIVES THEIR MOTHER A SCHOOL-GIRL UNIFORM !?

IDIOT STORE CLERK!

57

THESE, PERHAPS?

ER... MA'AM...?

UH...

UM...ER... P-PANTIES, PLEASE. PANTIES.

SQUIRM

SQUIRM...

OH DEAR, TERRIBLY SORRY! OH!

OH! OH-HO!

THEY'RE NOT FOR ME!!

I LOOK LIKE A BOY.

...THE MOST EMBARRASSING DAY OF MY LIFE.

5 O'CLOCK SHADOW

IF NO ONE NOTICES YOU'RE A ROBOT, I WIN!

SIR!

OKAY, LET'S TRY GOING OUTSIDE!

BOING BOING

STOP THAT!!

N'CHA!*

*SENBEI'S GREETING

COFFEE POT

DOCTOR **WHAT**!?

OH, DOCTOR SKUNK!

NONSENSE! I'M ONLY 28! SHE'S...MY SISTER!

YOUR DAUGHTER, SENBEI?

N'CHA!

HEY.

WHAT'S YOUR NAME?

YOU DON'T LOOK ALIKE AT ALL! GOOD FOR YOU, SWEETIE.

...

JUST BACK OFF!

WHAT FUNNY NAMES YOU BOTH HAVE!

WHAT HE SAYS!

WHAT'S MY NAME?

URK! YOUR NAME-- RIGHT! UM... ARALE! ARALE NORIMAKI!*

*ARALE: A SMALL RICE CRACKER   60

ENGINE OIL.

WHAT?

THWUMP

WHAT WOULD YOU LIKE, ARALE?

COFFEE FOR ME, THANKS.

WON'T I RUST?

WHEW.

J-JUICE! SHE'LL HAVE JUICE!

YOU DON'T LOOK LIKE YOU'RE IN JUNIOR HIGH.

PFFT

I'M STILL BRAND NEW!

SAY, HOW OLD ARE YOU?

HA HA, GOOD ONE! THIRTEEN! YOU'RE THIRTEEN!

61

YOU DON'T MIND, DO YA?

NOPE!

WHY NOT?

NO MORE QUESTIONS!

S-SOMETHING WRONG WITH HER NOSE?

ZOIK

SAY, YOUR NOSE...

?

NEITHER DO I! THIS IS A MANGA FOR CRYING OUT LOUD! A MANGA!

THUD

YOU DON'T HAVE NOSTRILS!

HEY, YOU'RE RIGHT! NO RUNNY NOSES!

CREAK

GOOD-BYE!
GOOD-BYE!
GOOD BYE-
BYE!

OKAY, THIS IS
GETTING SILLY.
LET'S GO HOME.

SCREEEECH

KIIIIN

WHAM

BOING

THAT...
THAT LITTLE
GIRL KNOCKED
OVER THE
CAR!

...

WOBBLE
WOBBLE...

OOPS.
MY
SHIRT
RIPPED.

Here Comes Arale!

MORNING, DOCTOR! TIME TO WAKE UP!

POP

DOCTOR!

SNAP

THUNK

GOOD MORNING!

WABOOM

66

MAN! I HAD THE **SCARIEST** DREAM.

SCHOOL STARTS TODAY, RIGHT?

HMM? OH, RIGHT...

DON'T DO ANYTHING ROBOT-LIKE, GOT IT?

YES, SIR!

ZZZIMMM

THAT'S WHAT I MEAN! STOP THAT!

67

PENGUIN VILLAGE MIDDLE SCHOOL

WELL, WELL. IF IT ISN'T DOCTOR NORIMAKI...

YO!

HA HA HA HA HA HA HA HA HA HA HA HA HA HA HA...

STILL, I'M SURPRISED. I DIDN'T KNOW YOU HAD SUCH A YOUNG SISTER.

YOU WERE SICK IN THE HOSPITAL ALL THAT TIME? POOR THING!

SHE'S MY DAUGHTER!

PSST! ACTUALLY...

OH!?

WEREN'T YOU QUITE YOUNG WHEN YOUR PARENTS PASSED AWAY?

BUT WAIT...

GAH

AH, THIS IS YOUR TEACHER, MS. YAMABUKI!

EXCUSE ME...

RATTLE

KRRRTCK

HER BROTHER SENBEI.

NICE... TO MEET YOU.

YES, AND THIS IS HER FATHER, DOCTOR--

YUP.

SO, YOU'RE MISS NORIMAKI?

WELL, CLASS WILL BE STARTING SOON.

BYE'CHA!

OH! RIGHT... SEE YOU LATER, THEN!

I WAS JOKING!

B-BUT YOU JUST SAID...!

YOU'RE A RARE BREED-- A TRUE PERVERT...

WHOO... PRETTY LADY.

WHEW

BAM

OH!

I HOPE ARALE'S GOING TO BE OKAY IN THERE.

GIVE ME A RIDE INTO TOWN, SENBEI! IT'S MATINEE DAY!

HUH? OH, IT'S YOU.

HEY! GREAT TIMING!

7th Grade

EVERYONE, PLEASE WELCOME ARALE NORIMAKI.

SHE'LL BE IN THIS CLASS STARTING TODAY.

LET ME OUT.

IN RETURN, YOU CAN BUY ME A TICKET.

YOU WANT OUT? BE MY GUEST!

VROOOOM

PHOOOO

...

HI! NICE TO MEET YOU.

MMRF MMRF

WHAAACHOO

KOOCHY-KOO.

...

WHAT'S YOUR NAME?

WHAT'S YOUR PROBLEM!?

HEE HEE

NO ONE SAID YOU HAD TO COME!

- Adults 1300
- Students 1100
- Children 800
- Infants 200

YOU'RE NOT SEEING THIS... ARE YOU?

HEY!

Nekotoraman vs. Nekotora-7

● Double Feature with Muscleman vs. Heidi of the Alps

HEEE

WHOA.

CLACK CLACKITY CLACKITY

CLACKITY CLINK CLINK

CHA-CHING

NOW, DOES ANYONE KNOW THE ANSWER?

THERE.

$$\sigma \div \square \triangle =$$
$$\frac{\times}{5} \div \female =$$
$$\square - \frac{\times}{5} =$$

SPLLT

NO. 1:
□○△×

NO. 2:
↕♀△×

NO.3...

THAT... THAT'S CORRECT!

I HAD TO LOOK UP THE ANSWERS...

MY!

ARALE JUST SUCCESSFULLY REMOVED THE FROG'S APPENDIX.

WHAT!?

FROG DISSEC-TION DAY IN BIOLOGY CLASS ...

NO MORE FUSSY, ME PROMISE. ME EAT OLD PEOPLE, TOO, NOW.

YOU PICKY EATER. SUN GOD NO LIKE. HIT YOU ON HEAD.

TURN AROUND! TURN AROUND!!

IDIOT! HE'S NOT OVER THERE!!

M E A N W H I L E . . !

BIING BOONG BIING BOONG

GIGGLE GIGGLE

WE MADE IT!

YAY YAY

BLAT

AAAH! MY SON!

THWACK

I SAID HE'S RIGHT BEHIND YOU!!

WHAT'S WITH HER?

...

HUH?

JUST LET GO, OKAY?

WHY'S SHE FOLLOWING ME!?

SHE'S THE NEW SUPER KID.

HUH?

HEH HEH... SHE SAYS YOU'RE FRIENDS!

SAYS *WHO!?*

'CAUSE WE'RE FRIENDS!

YEAH, WHY?

BAD!

DON'T HANG WITH US. WE'RE BAD, 'KAY?

75

I TOLD YOU TO STOP WEARING THAT STUFF!!

TARO!?

CUTE!

PLUB PLUB

HEH. YOU GOT GUTS, KIDDO.

IS SHE MAKING FUN OF YOU?

OR THIS IS YOUR FACE!! THAT ONLY HURT A LITTLE.

I LOVE HOW HE MAKES STUPID STUFF LOOK SO COOL.

GRRRR

BUT YOU BETTER WATCH IT!

CRUNCH

BROOO-PUT-PUT

LEGENDZ 1
The Tornado Comes!

RYUDO ELEMENTARY SCHOOL

FIFTH GRADE CLASS A

PIP

YOU WIN!

MY MERMAID TETTY WINS!

YAAY!!

RIRIKO YASUHARA

THAT'S AMAZING, RIRIKO!! IT'S YOUR 20TH STRAIGHT WIN!

HIDEAKI HIYAMA

I... I LOST AGAIN...

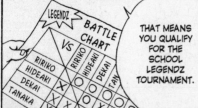

LEGENDZ BATTLE CHART

VS

	RIRIKO	HIDEAKI	DEKAI	TANA
RIRIKO		○	○	○
HIDEAKI	X		○	○
DEKAI	X	X		○
TANAKA	X	X	X	

THAT MEANS YOU QUALIFY FOR THE SCHOOL LEGENDZ TOURNAMENT.

90

91

TA-DA

RIRIKO! ONCE MORE FROM THE TOP!

LET'S YOU AND ME FIGHT!

WELL, IF RIRIKO WAS HIS OPPONENT, NO WONDER HE LOST.

Even I can't beat her.

I HEAR SHUNSUKE'S OLDER BROTHER IS REALLY GOOD AT LEGENDZ, THOUGH.

I WONDER IF HE'S OKAY. HE SEEMS REALLY DOWN...

PLIP

ERRR...

WITH 30 WINS AND 0 LOSSES !!

I JUST BATTLED YOU DURING LUNCH.

THERE'S A NEW STUDENT JOINING OUR CLASS TOMORROW!

HAVE YOU HEARD?

SHEESH

HEY! I FOR-GOT!

THE DATA FROM THESE CREATURES WERE SECRETLY ANALYZED AND RESEARCHED.

SOME OF THE RESULTS OF THAT RESEARCH WERE USED TO CREATE THE ULTIMATE HOBBY, LEGENDZ.

THE LEGENDZ ARE THOSE LEGENDARY MONSTERS, BUT LEGENDZ IS ALSO A GAME THAT PITS THEM IN BATTLE!!

SOUL FIGURE

THE DATA FROM THE LEGENDARY CREATURES ARE STORED IN HERE.

TALISPOD

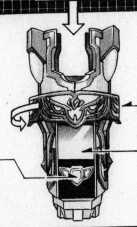

WHEN THE SOUL FIGURE IS SET INTO IT, THE LEGENDZ ARE REBORN. PLAYERS CAN RAISE THEM AND USE THEM FOR BATTLE.

■ JOGSWITCH

HAS THREE SETTINGS: REBORN (BATTLE), SOUL FIGURE (RAISE) AND EJECT (OFF)

■ MONITOR

DISPLAYS THE LEGENDZ'S DATA AND THE RESULTS OF BATTLE

■ SWITCH

SELECT/CANCEL BUTTON

97

I GOT MY WEREWOLF AS A BIRTHDAY PRESENT. IT'S MY PRIZED POSSESSION.

OF... OF COURSE I DO!!

DON'T YOU LOVE YOUR OWN LEGENDZ?

YOU CAN DO IT!

YEAH!

BUT...I ALWAYS LOSE THE BATTLES, AND I NEVER HAVE ANY FUN.

I WANT MY GUY TO WIN SOMETIMES.

WEREWOLVES DON'T RECOVER THEIR HIT POINTS UNLESS THEY'RE IN AN EARTH-WORLD SETTING.

FIRST OF ALL... THERE'S YOUR ENVIRONMENT.

YOU PUT HIM IN A FIRE WORLD!

AAAAH!! NO!

CHIK

UM... LIKE THIS?

SLAP

IF YOU RAISE IT WITH A LOT OF TLC, YOU'LL BE ALL RIGHT!!

I'LL TEACH YOU SOME TRICKS.

THIS IS HOW YOU DO IT...

DEKAI

BLIP BLIP

LEVEL UP!

BEEEEP

IT'S TRUE— WHEN YOU TAKE CARE OF IT, YOU START FEELING MORE AFFECTION FOR IT.

ALL RIGHT! NOW I'LL FEED HIM!

MY WEREWOLF JUST LEVELED UP!!

103

HEY!! SHUN-SUKE!

HEH HEH...

HO... HOSUKE...

Flinch

GYA AR

Y... YEAH.

I HEARD YOU LOST TO RIRIKO YASUHARA AGAIN TODAY. THAT RIGHT?

HEY...

!!

DUMMY!!

AAAH!!

KA-DA

KEEP IT UP, AND YOU'LL NEVER BE GOOD ENOUGH TO REPRESENT YOUR CLASS.

IF WE DON'T GET INTO THIS NEXT TOURNAMENT TOGETHER, YOU'RE GONNA MAKE ME LOOK BAD!!

GRAB

YOU'RE THE YOUNGER BROTHER OF THE GENIUS LEGENDZ WIELDER HOSUKE DEKAI!!

BUT...BUT... I JUST STARTED HAVING FUN RAISING MY WEREWOLF.

I WANNA BATTLE WITH MY OWN LEGENDZ...

?!

YOU GOT THAT?!

YOU'RE GONNA TAKE RIRIKO'S LEGENDZ TOMORROW!! THEN YOU CAN USE IT IN THE TOURNAMENT!

IF...

IF YOU GIVE UP YOUR LEGENDZ, YOU WON'T NEED TO TRY HARD!

WHAT HAPPENED? THOSE BANDAGES ON YOUR FACE...

SHUN-SUKE!!

WHAT ARE YOU SAYING!?

HUH?

WHAT DO YOU MEAN?

PLEASE, JUST LET ME USE YOUR LEGENDZ!!

I'LL COMPETE IN THE LEGENDZ TOURNA- MENT.

SHUN- SUKE... I DON'T KNOW WHAT YOU'RE TALKING ABOUT.

DAH

I RAISED TETTY MYSELF.

I CAN'T DO THAT.

WHAT'S THE MATTER, SHUN- SUKE? YOU'RE ACTING SO STRANGE!!

J-JUST GIVE ME YOUR LEGENDZ!!

I'M NOT GONNA LET YOU CALL MY YOUNGER BROTHER STRANGE!!

!!

ARE YOU ALL RIGHT, RIRIKO?

HMPH...

SLUMP

DON'T TAKE IT TOO HARD!!

Thanks.

GRAA

RIRIKO!

RI...

STAGGER

HEY!

HERE YA GO.

!!

SHUNSUKE'S GONNA PUT YOUR LEGENDZ TO GOOD USE IN THE TOURNAMENT.

DON'T LET IT GET YOU DOWN.

SHUNSUKE...

HEY!

!!

IF IT'S A LEGENDZ BATTLE, COUNT ME IN!!

WHAT'S UP?

YOU... YOU'RE THAT KID FROM—

DID YOUR LEGENDZ GET ANY STRONG- ER?

SHUP

YEAH!

GLARE

WHO'S THIS, SHUNSUKE? FRIEND OF YOURS?

HUH ?

UM ...

UM... WELL ...

112

114

COOL! IT'S A WIN-DRAGON!

Wow!

TA-

DAH

IS STRONG AGAINST

FIRE (VOLCANO)

IS STRONG AGAINST

WATER (STORM)

EARTH (EARTH-QUAKE)

IS STRONG AGAINST

IS STRONG AGAINST

WIND (TORNADO)

IS STRONG AGAINST

LET ME EXPLAIN!!

THIS IS BAD!!

A WINDRAGON? THIS COULD BE BAD...

RUSTLE

RUSTLE

LEGENDZ ARE CREATURES OF NATURE THAT MUST OBEY THE LAWS OF THE NATURAL WORLD. EACH ELEMENT IS STRONG AGAINST A DIFFERENT ELEMENT.

THEY'RE MAKING A WIND ELEMENT FIGHT AN EARTH ELEMENT!

I KNEW IT!!

Legendz for Beginners

THERE'S NO WAY HE CAN DEFEAT MY BROTHER'S TROLL...

IT'S IMPOS-SIBLE...

THIS BATTLE IS CLEARLY UNFAVOR-ABLE FOR THE WIN-DRAGON!!

EARTH BEATS WIND!

THAT MEANS...

?

NOT ONLY IS HE STRONGER, BUT HE'S UP AGAINST A WEAKER ELEMENT.

THE DATA SHOWED FROM THE BEGINNING THAT YOU HAD NO CHANCE!!

GET IT NOW? THIS IS BANRIKI'S POWER.

A HIT LIKE THAT MEANS GAME OVER, FOR SURE.

WHAT AMAZING POWER!!

126

AND ALL ACCORDING TO MY CALCULATIONS!

FACE FACTS!! I CREAMED YOU!!

HA HA HA HA !

WHAT DO YOU ...?

DO YOU ALWAYS GET WORKED UP OVER SUCH A TINY AMOUNT OF DAMAGE?

STRANGE.

Huh?

DIDN'T I TELL YOU?

ONE!? THE DAMAGE IS ONE!?

DAMAGE 01

HOW COULD YOU ONLY SUFFER ONE POINT OF DAMAGE AFTER BEING HIT BY THE ROCK BLOWGER?

132

YOU CAN'T MOVE !?

NO WAY!!

HOW CAN A TROLL BE HURT SO BADLY BY A WIND ATTACK?

ARRRRGH

THE WIND HE'S CREATING...

IT'S ENVIRON-MENTAL TRAIN-ING!!

WHOOOO

FLIP FLIP

HUH ?

...KEEPS YOU FROM MOVING !?